Beginning to Play
Mozart

Selected and Edited by MAY L. ETTS

CONTENTS

ISBN 978-0-7935-3460-9

Associated Music Publishers, Inc.

DISTRIBUTED BY
HAL•LEONARD® CORPORATION
7777 W. BLUEMOUND RD. P.O. BOX 13819 MILWAUKEE, WI 53213

FOREWORD

The "Beginning to Play" books have been planned to introduce to the piano student one great composer in each book. A number of his original, smaller compositions, ranging progressively from the easiest to those of moderate difficulty, have been selected to help the student become acquainted with the style of the composer of the particular volume.

"Beginning to Play" will not only be an introduction to MOZART but will offer the opportunity to become familiar with many of his beautiful masterpieces; to make a friend of MOZART and to continue studying his magnificent compositions long after this book has been completed.

M. L. E.

WOLFGANG AMADEUS MOZART
1756   1791

On January 27th, 1756, Wolfgang Amadeus Mozart, one of the greatest geniuses the world has ever known, was born in Salzburg, Austria.

The little Wolfgang revealed such extraordinary musical abilities, that when he was four years old his father Leopold began to instruct him in clavier playing.

Leopold Mozart was an excellent musician, an admirable composer and a sensible man, possessing the sound judgement needed to undertake the education of such a talented child.

At the age of five, little Wolfgang began his career by composing minuets which his father wrote down for him. His sister Nannerl, 5 years older, also was remarkably talented, and Wolfgang developed great skill very rapidly, so the father decided to take his gifted children on a concert tour, starting with Munich and Vienna. They became the sensation of the day and were received and entertained by royalty.

Even while he was traveling, Wolfgang's education in music continued. In his sixth year, he began the study of the violin, soon adding instruction on the organ. He acquired facility in the technic of both instruments with extraordinary quickness.

In 1763, when Wolfgang was seven years old, he and his sister went to Paris where they played before the royal family. This was followed by two brilliant and successful concerts. While Mozart was in Paris, his first compositions were published. They were four Sonatas for Harpsichold with accompaniment of violin and flute.

The reception given to the Mozarts was even more enthusiastic in London. Their stay in England was a long one, and there Mozart studied with an excellent Italian singer, soon mastering the Italian style of singing. He excited great admiration by his sight reading of works of Bach, Handel, and others.

The Mozarts returned to Salzburg in 1765. Wolfgang's compositions at this time included more sonatas and his first symphonies. A period of serious study followed during which time he composed his first oratario and an opera. He also appeared as conductor in a concert at which his "Solemn Mass" was performed.

In 1769, the thirteen year old Mozart was taken to Italy where his genius was immediately recognized. In Bologna he was admitted to membership in the celebrated Philharmonic Academy, passing with ease an examination which would have appalled many mature musicians.

In Milan, he was commissioned to write an opera which was so enthusiastically received that it was given more than twenty performances, the first one conducted by the young composer. One of the older musicians of Milan said, "This boy will cause us all to be forgotten".

The success of his opera Idomeneo, written a number of years later, definitely secured Mozart's position as a dramatic composer. In the operas "Figaro" and "Don Giovanni", he fully developed his inexhaustible genius. He was a master of every form of composition, and was greatly responsible for the increased brilliance and color of orchestral sound through the addition of new instruments and the introduction of fresh tonal combinations.

Mozart composed 679 works during the short thirty-five years of his lifetime. There are a number of beautiful operas in addition to those named previously, dozens of sonatas including 22 for piano, 55 concertos for various instruments, 49 symphonies, masses, oratorios, works for many other instrumental combinations, and a great number of short, very attractive piano solos, some used in this book. There are others, more difficult, that you will enjoy studying and playing as you advance.

I hope you will become so interested in Mozart that you will want to read some of the many fascinating books about him and listen to some of the many recordings of his works.

MINUET in C

MINUET in F

Allegretto

6

MINUET and TRIO

LITTLE DANCE

ALLEGRO in B♭

MINUET

LITTLE SONG

Andante con moto

MINUET in B♭

14

ALLEGRO

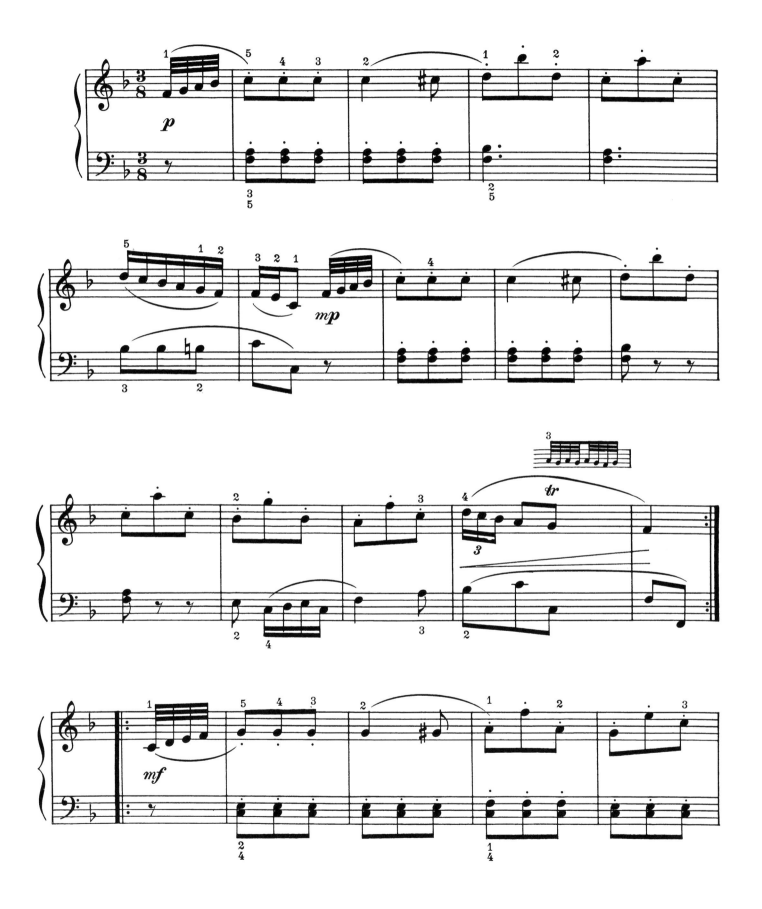

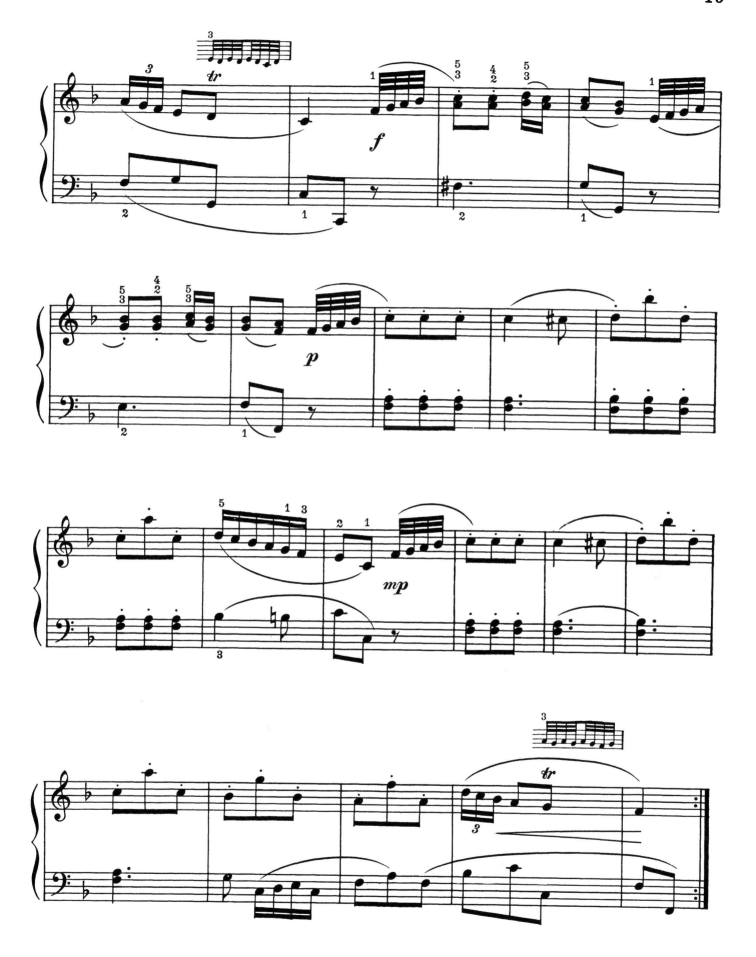

MINUET

AIR

MINUET in F

AIR in E♭

RONDO in F

MINUET in C

Allegretto

MINUET in Eb

COUNTRY DANCE

TRIO
Poco più mosso

RONDO in D

POLONAISE

ANDANTINO

RONDO in C